The Colour of Flight

The Colour of Flight

Linda Waybrant

To Janet
enjoy!

Linda Waybrant

Wolsak and Wynn . Toronto

Typeset in Helvetica, printed in Canada on Zephir Laid by The Coach House Printing Company, Toronto

Front cover photo: Linda Waybrant
Cover design: Stan Bevington
Author's photo: Suzanne Waybrant

The author wishes to acknowledge and thank the following people for their support and friendship: Allan Briesmaster, Mary Ellen Csamer, Albert Fuller, Pierre L'Abbé, Kathy Waybrant, Suzanne Waybrant, Frank Young, and those participating in Phoenix Poetry Workshop.

Some of these poems first appeared in *Prairie Fire, Event, Poetry Canada*, and *Fireweed*. Seven of the poems in the section titled "Father" won *Prairie Fire*'s Long Poem Contest, 1995.

The publishers gratefully acknowledge support from The Canada Council and The Ontario Arts Council which has made publication of this book possible.

Wolsak and Wynn Publishers Ltd.
Don Mills Post Office Box 316
Don Mills, Ontario, Canada, M3C 2S7

Canadian Cataloguing in Publication Data

Waybrant, Linda, 1957-
  The Colour of Flight
Poems.

ISBN 0-919897-50-9
I. Title.
PS8595.A88C6 1996   C811'.54   C96-931122-2
PR9199.3.W389C6 1996

if the past is no longer tomorrow
and the moon in December is no longer cold
what name will you invent for yourself

what season is this
now that you realize the birds were not truly birds
and the trees
      well
        they were never trees

our symbols were never entrusted to us
our inheritance was never the coming harvest

                          — *Albert Fuller*

for
Albert
Kathy
&
Suzanne

CONTENTS

1 DRUXY'S

DRUXY'S

1.
a man speaks on tv about his writing
tells us that some of it is factually true that it wasn't just
in a book that he wrote that his tongue
up & down her flesh ran no stopping
delicious sugar-coated lover
met at the intersection of two well-known streets
he wanted to talk about her hair
say more than his book with his hands shape of his lips
going over the words
in person how the mouth opens stays open drags
its syllables until the end
of the word the rhythm of breathing in & out of loving
making sweet beads of sweat
on tv to an interviewer as he's interviewed about his novel
that he says is yes some biography

2.
a woman knows this tall man
has met this man read his book
has spoken
the heat & steam from their coffee the cold air outside
the warmth inside
oh she says this book about a woman he wanted
made
love to
in the dark
a fictional woman not real

3.
their connection involves a knife
a tall man meeting a woman talking
& murmuring to a woman
a woman falling in love clean
through to the heart
galloping the heart
contacting
light pouring
or jabbing the heart the pancreas
a single lung left to power a small house
their situation different houses
the difference
the blue & red & blue
of the knife going in the life coming out
a tall man with a knife
a tall man without a knife
a tall man with the hint of a knife a summer sky or evening
not this endless thief winter on & on this barren winter
never a morning
through the window of a coffee shop
not now
not her

4.
but a fictional woman
is
between
them
his long legs reaching out from under the table
hips swivelling round
laughing coughing

14

ANOTHER STORY BOOKSHOP

164 DANFORTH AVE. (AT BROADVIEW)

WELCOMES POETS

ROBERT HILLES

(1994 Governor General Award Winner)
author of
NOTHING VANISHES

and

LINDA WAYBRANT
author of
THE COLOUR OF FLIGHT

THURS. 20th FEB. 6:30 - 8:30

For more information, please call 462-1104

somewhere
they had something
going

5.
oh she says she
is disappointed in this book
this ghost of a book
· this weak unpalatable broth of adolescent memory & worse she says
he's on the tv
lunging at details finger by finger
his head thrown back he confides to the audience
he ignores the audience he ignores her
on & on she is ignored in every page with every gesture every word
as he speaks of a character he met on a street while he sat in a bar
alone
always alone
the stale night inside a dirt bar
at 2 a.m. coffee next door

6.
she met him at Druxy's
late it was too late
& where was she going & why the tears who's buying he said
an address a phone number because she told him for no reason
except the grey endless days start
at the same time end at the same time
where does it end
even if she goes back to her husband

7.
was there ever a possibility
ever a valentine
viewed sideways or upside down in an alley on a wall

15

bleeding pink on slushy sidewalks
honking & squelching time spent freezing in hell
sentiment inside words
solid walls
limbs eyes ears nostrils for him & her each for each

he is a guy who says he uses knives to cut valentines
cut along the dotted lines he does not

it is *his* novel after all
it is *his* fictional character
after all is said & done she loved him
not he her
they met
in a coffee shop
then she went home to her husband
excluding her phone calls & letters

8.
it is the scene about the fictional woman & a window that he does not
talk about halfway through the chapters & pages a night
he climbs through her fictional window
the window not locked waiting
he was waiting for her
he had waited so long for her
to come back

9.
these characters did not meet in a place where they could stretch out
stretch their bodies
brush against each other with some part of the body
a foot touching another foot lingering
her thigh touching his thigh lingering

16

& he came through the window
& waited
until she was asleep
curtains the open valentine with his mouth
chapter 16

10.
she is at home on her new couch alone
this book is offensive she frowns
these characters thin
she does not finish the book
his tongue a hair's breath away

11.
the tall man says he's often in a bar
a barstool with his name he winks
a home away from home he says
& a beer goes down
& another
glass
smudged chipped glass
holding liquor
holding his own
sliding down
in a bar
it took years to get out of the bar
to write these words he says
hair greasy
hand bruised
eye glasses taped
in a bar
at the back
on the floor

12.
a snowy night when she had left had begun
to walk straight ahead
blindly until it seemed she had walked directly to him
above her a loping grin
a chair floating coffee dancing
a man looking at her
sitting with her
telling her
like a knife
suddenly
she felt
cut
open

she is unhappy
looks away
looks out to the yard
the fence & the small climbing rose bright red buds
closed tight
it's not all factual he says on tv before it's turned off
before the dark of night the dark of last call
two for last call
alone
so many nights so many days
a book where his tongue licks
the salt of her armpit as she sleeps
the ocean in his mouth
a nuzzling small tongue print
soft
the mark of his love
based on truth he says not looking at the camera
only his legs reaching out from under him

lying
open

13.
as it turns out
this fictional character is
awake
although he does not know
he will not know
not his intention to make her wake up
he does not let her wake up
she can not open her eyes
they can't open
but a fictional character is
that very situation

so this fictional woman
not by words
leaves her window open
she does not use words to make this window
open
to push up a window
unlock
lift
there is nothing but she
an open window
she opened

14.
the other woman stopped reading the book
stopped at the window left
wide to evening sunset
light streaming

bringing night & the feel of tongue on skin
the fictional woman feels
his tongue dotting lines of connection
feels her heart
feels him against her
this fictional woman is

15.
as he nods / disagrees on tv his hair bobbing
his body flat
his space two-dimensional
the woman watching
her space
on & on

16.
the valentine is fiction
the valentine is a fictional woman feeling
feeling a cut to the heart
the cutting towards the heart
air to the heart
hear it beating
beating & drumming
out
her fictional heart
a valentine thick with desire
choked with desire
the dry glint of a knife brandished page after page
on paper the heat
on paper his tongue touching her skin
paper
edges
made round

20

feel his desire for her
feel her desire for him
swollen unspent desire

feel
ever
unthawed

II FATHER

IF SOMEONE PUTS YOU IN AN EMPTY FREEZER
CLOSES THE LID
YOU LISTEN TO YOUR BROTHER'S FAR-AWAY VOICE

you get small
you get real small
can hear what he's saying but
you don't call out
wait
a very long time

when you are small
you can lie down on the floor of the freezer
you'll hear two people talking
about what should happen next
if one is your father   he'll say
I'm going to the kitchen to make coffee
if one is your brother   he'll say
let her out
you can squeeze your eyes very tight
look up at the lid
think: Orion comes out at night
             my brother is crying

because you imagine water filling the box
             & feel yourself slip over & through it
             circle slowly round & round
because you hear talking
             & start to count backwards
because you know the lid is lifting
             edged apart by the white tips of wave crests
because you have stretched out in this lean night
because you are one hand print from light

you don't say a thing

& when you tell your story
it will start with the bird you found under a red maple
you'll say   Dead birds have very small eyes.
          If I had a blanket
          I would cut it into the shape of this bird
          take a ribbon
          & wrap its silent body
          attach a note & put a mark on the tree.

          Two days later I'd dig it back up: prove
          feathers remain soft
          skin gets cold.

          How long do you think he left me in there?

& when she tells her story
she says   fish in small bowls
                gold fish   wrapped wrapped in soft tissue
                one eye left to see free

see the unimaginable—
a child fitting inside easily she climbed into
                        the white
                        the dumb white
                                        of trust
                a child's story: always a door out
                to the empty space of understanding

a conversation on a drive home
one person speaking to another
a horizon with no beginning
no end

we ate doughnuts in the car while my niece cried

because it was so late
because we liked the cowboy song on the radio
because it was cold outside
how cold do you think it will get?

without light

without heat

because when she tried to spread herself out
she hit her head

landscape   too often defined by what it lacks

27

a story—
of a small dark place
where a child tries to keep something warm

imagining white

remembering at age 12 a bathing suit splashed with orange flowers
my hair long
my body stretching up
unfolding in the summer's heat
gaining depth in scented air

that winter my loves were hockey players
a chaste apprenticeship
of rules
& matching names to numbers
of wins & losses
home & away
one player chosen to receive letters
to wait for
before a game
I remember borrowing my sister's shiny striped coat
the wet November sleet
the fresh cut above his left eye / his long eyelashes
how having his name scrawled across pastel-shaded paper
meant something promising to me

now imagining the breathless austerity of snow
landscape unencumbered by the girth & wealth of summer—
in my favourite bathing suit
my father's drunk friend grabbing my legs
pinching me hard between my legs
laughing
as I pulled & ran away

perfect stillness of white

unlike the arena's bristling dry air
swish of blades slivering ice
crack of pucks against boards
& behind the "reds" a place named "standing room"
so close to the action
so crowded & warm—
how to speak this unnamed shame:
the man behind me
touching me
following me

memories as green washes & waves swirl round stars—
dance riotously
freed in the night

imagining the simplicity of white

the aloneness of white

absence   coloured white

MARCONI INC.

out of a father's closet
          with boxes of transistor tubes
          pulled from under the four squat legs of a tv
is sharp memory—

          of fear's quick flash
          in a parking lot
          at a front office job
          for a company
          that bankrupted

          there is a car
          kids climbing from front & back
          the car is deep & black & cool
          the doors are not locked
          & when a stranger confidently seats himself inside
          only the oldest of the children thinks danger

          the stranger smiles
          gets the kids to jump out of the car
          follow his white shirt into the brick building
          down the hall
          turn left
          find their Dad
          hard at work
          on a Saturday—

memory heavier than the shopping bags of odd socks
          pills
          coats
          blankets
          & of late
          the dishes from the cupboards of a government bachelor

31

the day an apartment gets cleared out
after a death

& even though the older kids
stopped going with their father
stopped sitting in cars that were dented & hot
beside entrances marked "men"
windows closed tight

& even though the younger kids would get out of the cars
start walking home
silent beside noisy highways

this memory alone
        of a child
        looking a man straight in the eye
        a man looking back
        acknowledging fear
        taking fear away

surfaces
& a kind of waiting
unshuts abruptly

C. W.   (1932 - 1991)

each fine run of hair trimmed into line
one quarter inch above a jacket's collar
soft clean yellow spring jacket
unzipped
as he slowly makes his way down a busy street
towards an apartment
that was cleared out three weeks ago

   this must be a dream
she shouts into the restaurant
to the person behind the door
   in dreams
   story lines flip
   into old story lines
   lines you don't necessarily want to repeat

but if this is not a dream
we have to stop him from going to his apartment
that is empty
of food
of furniture
of letters
& photos kept for years at the bottom of a green garbage bag

because if he goes back to his apartment
it will always be empty
no matter
which dream
this dream of two stories:
one of his death
one of the thought of his death

& before anyone can answer
before the ordering of french fries & carrots & prime rib
before any door is opened
this dream of story lines
ends
flat
down the middle
of every single day
that I spend mourning a man I didn't want to know
knew
by the way he arranged jars above his sink
each one standing taller than the next—
the pencils & elastics
the cards of dark thin thread

ABOUT A CHAIR

broken
not by him
he is too old
bent
with knees that need coaxing into their sitting position
          a jaw that holds pain like a cradle

about a chair
balanced on his finger
obscenities of beds   neighbours
          dogs   places of employment
paraded in front of the wife
          the mother
          the morning she settled into
dreaming practicalities
          as the soft green of a small new leaf
                    the colour of a single leap of grass
                    the green of daughters & sons
                    chasing water sprinklers
                    back & forth
                    outside on the front lawn
                    of a two-storey home
                    in the suburbs near ravines
                    & parks
                    & secret places
          is damned

about a chair
smashed against the floor
          hurled against the wall
          thrown down the stairs
hits the wall   splinters
cracks—
plaster applaudingly cascading in a downpour

35

of home construction
　　　　of real estate & dust
odds & ends
strewn out—
the finishing nails
the bolts & brackets
the end of the chair that he hates

hates the support rungs & the thick green paint
　　　　over & over again
　　　　years of brush strokes & the extended family
one chair tossed into the air
launching
a statement of the unbridled
　　　　sailing
　　　　into the future

until impact

a chair
in a green hospital room
him mumbling details of swollen pulpy jaw
　　　　cancer jaw
　　　　a pin throbbing in an ochre jaw
about a chair he moved to the window
or out to the balcony
or like he said
about a chair to help him tumble into a 17-storey drop

about a chair
broken
evidence that chairs hit people
might hit her
might get smashed right on her head
broken
not by him
because he is too small
with knees that need persuasion
            a jaw that suffers the pain

IF HE CALLS
YOU CAN BET HE'S BEEN DRINKING
YOU CAN BET A BOTTLE'S HALF GONE

he phoned to continue a conversation started 20
maybe 25 years ago
from the Friday just past
he said I kept banging my head
when I was 1½ years old
that my head was round
round like a bowling ball
a perfect head
round like his
round like the earth
so much salt water to float my head around & around in

he said he only slapped my mom
& he can't remember hitting me
did he hit me or slap me
he wanted to know
he found her in bed with another man
& he didn't hit her he slapped her
that I shouldn't put the blame on him
that she didn't hear me crying
& there were fleas
clothes piled up
socks needing mending
oceans that were so red they hurt his eyes

& something had to be done
something had to be done about what was wrong he yelled
he yelled so loud that I started to sweat
& my head pounded—
he told me he was getting angry
he told me he didn't do a thing

five kids
can't understand
how would I know
then he hung up

but there's always another phone call
& another

& the phone
never swims free of the reeling
round
the smallest globe
the rings & rings of pain sketched as history

connection
by cord
choking blind cord

THERE ARE CATS I SEE IN YELLOW CAGES
& THEY ARE TALKING ABOUT HOW THESE DAYS
ARE GONNA BE THEIR LAST—
I HAVE TO PUT ON SUN GLASSES
TO HIDE THE SALT

I still don't know the story
I'm still running down the stairs
sort of sideways
looking up
but going down to the basement
get my shoes
go to school
something like that
my father was yelling
so early in the morning
about the cats
he was yelling at me
I had to get the younger kids away
& they wouldn't
they kept telling me he had the cats

I put the dead kittens in my drawer
I put the dead cat in a box in my drawer
I put a note in the drawer

      tonight
      after work
      I will look in the cages they keep
      for lost cats
      walk by the road
      call my cat's name

40

I still don't know the story
how many cats were left
who it was by the curb
if there were any marks
or what I did to make him pick up the kitten
the one with the black hat
& throw it
I don't remember
        my story
        is that the vet is doing tests
        on my nine-year-old cat
        missing for a week
        it will cost he said

to keep your cat from dying
in the kitchen
in the backyard
in a box under your bed
I don't know the whole story
because I didn't come home at lunch
& I didn't ask

        I have to leave my cat with him
        because she's not eating
        & her eyes look real sad
        I'll pay

NOTHING EVER WARM AGAIN
　　—Patrick Friesen, "Starry Night"

(for Pierre)

our fathers led us to water

& let go

our fathers held us
their hands round our wrists
crossing streets
through traffic
across parking lots
to grocery stores & shoe stores
licorice &
sweet green grapes
our tiny fingers
small arms
reaching up
as we walked
ran
out
towards
a flawlessly blue sky

& a grey lake—
a wide sad lake
too cold for swimming

our fathers
let go

42

fathers that need a chance
a chance to lift their children above the cold scream of waves
to hold a child's head above
every drowning
to stop
the tears
            a chance to revive a memory—
            a coasting & whirling of fresh seeds
            navigating the edge
                    the line between daylight
                    & the gasping for breath
                    a free fall
                    gliding
                    lofty
                    to a landing

III   TRAINS CROSSING

I HAVE RIDDEN THE SUBWAY WHILE IT RAINED TORRENTS

> *The true meanings of words are always*
> *down in the intonation.*
> —Josef Skvorecky, *The Bass Saxophone*

& knew you were watching me
the leaves on my dress turning a shade deeper
as each open-air station pulled away
the smell of cold slipping round my legs

I have heard your emptiness
your silence big & aching as the purple sky

I breathe back
let's have each other right now
welcome this beige & plastic morning
in the corner seat
send buttons into flights
line the floor with wool
feed the space where loons cry
& you lie at 2 a.m. with someone you're not sure you love

I have ridden the subway while thunder
applauded the sky
& knew you were waiting

A CLOUDY DAY
A MAN IN A GREY SWEATER NOW WHISTLING

(for Frank)

it is the city that he lives in
it is this morning as he walks because he enjoys walking
maybe to the store
to meet a friend for lunch
breezes past the houses on a quiet street
a brisker walk in cooler weather

like her
he started his day reading
except it was early when he walked to the bus stop & got the paper
she has had it delivered
& is only starting her day now

but it is not anything to do with the paper or the walk
that he'll remember for such a long time
it is how she gathered her pale nightgown with one hand
& stepping out
reached with the other:
        barely visible—the slope of her breasts
        behind the scooped neck
        its lace edging
        as she bent to the ground

that made him smile
& catching her eyes with his
startled her with their merriment—

48

a curve
a soft warm luxury of mornings spent under flannel sheets
sun streaming as two people whisper
a glimpse of skin
she hadn't meant—
its intimacy a rare jewel in the light of this late morning
the lines of protocol
both crossed & made to disappear:
a single realized moment

she will quickly close her door
aware of her own heartbeat & an embarrassed flush
she'll place the unwound package on a nearby chair
turn towards a mirror

A TRAIN CROSSING

trains whistle: birds on their wings
of metal
& sky
rain clouds
rolling in
rumbling
the sky
darkens slowly
thunder
signalling
trains crossing
the wooden arm that has come down

she waits in her car listening to the radio
she feels tired
as a man holds a lifeless child
a woman breaks down & cries
staring straight ahead
she reads her own name in the alphabet that streams by
lately it seems she has to try so much harder
to be who she wants to be—
& the songs of a girl waiting on a boy
across a terrain of broken bottles cigarette ends
& the upstart of wild flowers

she isn't twenty years old anymore
she was never sweet sixteen
never held a ticket
to board a train
somewhere out of here
never the sort of woman to surprise a running train & win

or lose herself
in the sound of one train
& the hidden sound of another

two died
in the bright yellow sunshine as a bird took cover
out of the path of one train & into another's
singular path

she is tired
miles of rail slashing across & dividing
her pleated skirt her soft red sweater sticking to her skin
parallel rails
one direction
nothing more
than to acknowledge the three colours: red green & caution
today she is dressed in red

she continues to peer through her car window
presses her head against her sleeve & wipes sweat from her brow
she is dressed too warmly for a spring day
inside her car it is too hot
if it doesn't rain very soon ...

from the train a worker appears
he swings his legs up & over
& grasps a door
he turns to the sound of a car's brief hoot
waves to the traffic with a grin

she waves back
imagines that her red clothed arm catches his eye

13 stories below a cement wall
6 men 5 women & 3 children
all shading their eyes
squinting from the glare off water
lounging on deck chairs
lotioning their arms to a brown & freckled glow
the buzz of insects drowned by motors
the city 2½ hours south west
engines pumping sweet inspiration
propelled by what's under foot
locked in on four sides
waiting to be lifted above where they were
get to a place surrounded by the hum of a primary season

lake rushing in
playing saucily
the slap of infant waves at a hand-in-glove standstill
boats ever poised & ever positioned for a better view:
a wider circle
of water
this distance upward
not the actual journey
yet no less—
to rise
to feel we can begin anew

BLUE BIRD

(for Sean)

said to him
take this old picture
I painted it when I was sixteen
your age now plus four months
it's a bird
it's blue and is mostly dots
I didn't know it was a bird when I painted it
only when I held it up later
& saw that a head was missing
a small head with two long flowing feathers
stuck right on top
oh & the eyes weren't there either
one big
one small
I put them on after that fancy hat

take this bird picture
these paints
maybe add what you think is missing
start with the time between us
the space water takes up
when it squeezes from my eyes your eyes
the distance our memories have crawled

maybe you can put in the other wing
I don't make wings so good
I only made the bird one
paint it on big
paint it red or something
make the wing a rainbow that stretches
clear over to the other wing

make it magic
then if we wanted
the bird could fly
right off the paper
whoosh over to me
& speedy back to you

yah
take this bird
I made it for you

IF I HAD A CHILD
MY SISTER & I WOULD HAVE FOUR ALL TOGETHER
4½ IF WE COUNT THE ONE GROWING IN HER NOW

(for Cindy)

some women grow their babies in wheat fields
tall & straight
yellow stringy hair & solemn faces

some women grow children from spring seeds
to stand watch
like scarecrows waiting to be held

some women build their babies in factories
glass beads for eyes
backs that can carry almost anything

my sister grows hers from a soup pot
when she's not looking they eat the cat's food
add crooked stars to the wallpaper

55

> *oh, it beckons and beckons*
> *and I want to go back*
> > —Robert Service, *The Spell of the Yukon*

(for Debra)

if she went into the kitchen   I didn't notice
I was saying—
a place that takes in its own air
the way an airplane lifts into the sky
a light sweat   a last swallow   rush—
then the surprising swoop of   maybe
wings unrealized   a jump that stays up
breath   held   in
it's something I don't understand   but can feel—
feels so tangy   so enormous
as if nothing can ever be taken away again:
a stretch of wide autumn
tall & unbounded

the gold   burnt umber   turquoise & jagged rock
beckon & beckon
they stand tip-toed &
amply skied

if she left at that point   I missed it
don't want to get our stories mixed together
is what she said later
she was thinking   I might not be left with my own:
naming will route this splendid place home—

it will be too small
for this threadbare child

this timeworn child carrying the history of poverty
recognizing herself

protecting what is hers

a conversation begun when a father
came home
finished when a father left
in his car
to return to business
after lunch
a conversation between son & father—
eight-year-old son with something more to add

he ties his shoelaces
buttons his coat
closes the door
in time to see his father's long silver car skirt the corner
of a flickering slowpoke street
he runs
runs faster because there is something more
something he'd like to say
about the plumage of apple trees

that child
          so sure of his words
          the spectrum of love
comes up empty
on a grassy boulevard
the sun making a question mark of the meandering road

it does not seem possible it could end in any other way

THE POLLEN HAS LANDED
& I DIDN'T TELL MY BROTHER

(for Jamie)

that the hillside overlooking the baseball game was steep
the men down there hot
one by one were shedding their shirts
that I sat
far enough away to stare
        I didn't say I sneezed four times in a row
each explosion inching me closer
& making dandelions leave buttercups on my dress

        my brother's foot was still broken that day & his
soon to be wife talked about their
soon to be built house
one crack in the west wall foundation repaired overnight
the mortgage decided last May

        I didn't tell him lilacs bloomed in my pockets
18 babies slept at the pet shop
that lately the sun had been up early
        I didn't tell my brother
there's a photo of me holding him up
our shoes scuffed at the toes & our hair
bleached to the same shade of simplicity
        that the blue sky
is bigger than both of us
with or without the clouds

DOMESTIC

watching her run only an hour ago
the wind making light of her summer dress
the grass hiding the slope that made her tumble
suitcases   flung forward
& still in gear
I called out to ask if she was ok
hearing my sister laughing or maybe the sound of tears

it's a short flight to Chicago
not including packing the bare shoulder dress
        shoes wrapped in tissue
        & a phone call as she waits to board her plane—
talk of the weekend
my plans to paint walls
alone that night
& the next
a husband who'd be working or out late
& something else
although not spoken—
a forgotten conversation
the same misplaced request

telling her like a chorus to have fun
take care
confirming when she'll return
which flight
which airline
details offered & heard
again
as comfort
a way of caring

both of us too often alone
not with our music & photos & cats in windows
not in our yards with sun soaked flowers & seed for birds
but alone in the day's movements:
the steps between awakening & opening the door to sunlight
or washing the dishes
putting away the dishes
hanging shirts to dry
& boiling water for tea

we share this daily pace
each in our own homes
although she lives alone & I don't
we shop for food together
sometimes build shelves
make each other's calls:
get to Chicago for a friend's art show
spare no change

placing the receiver down
I pick up where I left off—
empty something that is full
close something still open
vaguely waiting for my husband to come home
recalling: late snacks
                   library books
                   talk of what's been repaired
remembering how often his body slips into sleep
as I speak my version of the day
& lately the coming together:
pleasure
one at a time

our mouths uttering no words & sharing no kisses
holding back
& too often
plausible reasons

tonight being alone seems like all there ever is
the water here
tasting of tears

IV A BLUE DRESS

a small animal's winter coat
a small animal with a sharp nose
baby mink perhaps
a tiny fox
or a long elegant mouse
stroked up & down
& an ivory bracelet
carved flowers & leaves
on & off my wrist in a second

gifts from my aged aunts
aunts that attached
plastic flowers to Sweetheart soap
with pearls & satin
chorus girl aunts
named after the men they loved
widowed
childless
quietly filling the rest of their years:
crafts learned at church
jars of Avon
tissues of lace
powdery embroidered pillows

they offered a petite animal
a pale garden
to furtively make games with
touch:
a cut of fur
a bone handcuff

not that it was easy to accept gifts
not easy to accept anything
from anyone
so that hiding them seemed the right thing to do

GIFTS (2): A BLUE DRESS

       she said this blue is your colour
a perfect colour for you she said from the hospital bed
near the window on a warm sunny day
       she said your slip is showing
as she tied a frayed ribbon into a bow
or maybe my hem was hanging loose
maybe there was a tear in my dress where the sash joined the cloth
& if I kept my arms straight
no one would see how the dress was
slowly unravelling

       it will be all right she said
let me smooth out the waist—
cover your slip
that was torn
that was dirty
that was falling apart

underneath this skirt of blue
underneath this bright blue cotton

GIFTS (3): GRANDMOTHER'S HEIRLOOMS

                a china figurine
                the stalks of silver between double folded linen
                the photo of a young girl
blushed
gently
                & rooms of smooth porcelain
white & gold furniture
ache of mahogany
                the bristly wool   crisscrossed hardwood—
games for the eyes while
white potatoes   peas
a well-cooked roast
were brought to the table

                the onyx ring
scripted in my name
our name
                in a drawer smelling of lavender
the velvet wrapped beads—
prisms that danced on your dresses your ears
your size five shoes

keepsakes you'd call them
smiling
as you cleared breakfast dishes
returning the small blue pitcher
                a holder for orange juice
                cool fog marking colder liquid
that waited for me
on the top shelf of the fridge
every short visit—
carefully I'd fill the glass with the petal leaves
beside the tulip spoon
on a placemat of lace

GIFTS (4): GRANDFATHER'S FUNERAL

I have only a few memories of my grandfather
they are not reliable:
a band of flowers
one for each grandchild—
seven in 1965
maybe they were pink rosebuds
near to where his hands were folded

I had to be lifted to look closely at them
secretly chose one to be mine
as he lay there
asleep I said to someone

but knowing this wasn't true
knowing even then how innocent words had impact
feeling ashamed that I had lied in this quiet place
where my grandfather waited
for the door to close—
my flower safely with him on the inside

I think we went by streetcar to a button factory
where he held me up
to his friends
his old colleagues
told them I was his granddaughter
as if that mattered
as if it counted for something big

WE WERE VERY SCARED WHEN HER FATHER DIED
I WAS SIX THEN & KATHY WASN'T BORN YET

my mother doesn't talk about a lot of things
but she told me she hated the photo
of my grandfather
enlarged for her last Christmas
a dark shadow shortening the days
until he'd be waving from the hospital's seventh floor

it was a family picture
grandpa holding all the new babies
my dad loosely hugging her
all of us smiling

it was way before my father ever hit her
way before his eyes turned real green
because the white part was so red
before my sister & I shared the double bed
& could cry & pray & sleep without making a sound

she said grandpa was too sick to come down
made us stand outside & look up at a shiny window
during the drives home
she wouldn't say a thing—
one by one she'd hand over stuff for us to play with:
we bent amber hair pins
petted velvet high heels
clicked her purse open then shut—

each one of us holding watch through the back window
as a fast grey road
chased
unrelentingly:
only a sharp turn gave this tail the slip
but so briefly
yet just as suddenly
time
with a few words about a photo
played this same trick:
listening
as she cried very softly
her dark curls bouncing
I heard her speak a child's name
I saw that child nod
take her hand & look ahead

how like us to remember the details of single events
& map them together—
the coming from one place to arrive at another:
to be here at this ocean
having driven on this road
walked this winding pathway
around the bare limbs of the tamaracks
straight into a slew of pearly-everlastings
as if stepping through time

the children (3 girls & 3 boys) have grown so tall & thin
the boys younger
still decorating themselves with towels & helmets & stick-on tattoos
the girls
now self-consciously girls
long hair swinging as they toss their heads
eye themselves in mirrors
looking to make a match
in a new pair of jeans
a gauzy dress
lipstick
the first softening—
the wild swell of breasts

each child's birth not unlike the first—
the call to her mother from a room of phone booths in France
soixante-dix Madame said
& we counted by tens to make sure
asked what her name would be
spoke it over & over
laughing about things we'd teach her

in tents under Pegasus
in sleeping bags heated by fire-warmed rocks
the lost & found stories

we watch how she paces her family
deflects sarcasm
encourages her sister's red face
into tears
flipping back those words her sister remains defiant—
a morning years ago I heard her singing to her dolls
the only early riser in a cottage sleeping eight

the 4- & 5-year olds
sun-lightened hair
mischief-speckled eyes
nose to nose with second cousins
the questions
the bullying
the deals
a parent's deal for a hamster—
sleep in your own room
my father's lap
his two knees
not the only territory to be staked out

& a small chair
plush & furry
for the baby because he can walk—
that wide grin of recognition
as he sits then carries his chair

we have arrived at this place with the children
standing still
time is bending into circles:
we are at this ocean again
buoyant in this water
gathering these smooth rocks
choosing pink granite like the last time
we walk among familiar trees
hear the crunch of last winter's needles

these children leading us around our own geography

the desire to share our lives
a gentle pull
or suddenly fierce: those without sons or daughters to care for
assured of rain & sun
our arms ever ready to catch a fall

surely we would not fail
given the chance

V BEGINNING FROM THE MIDDLE OF DARKNESS

EXODUS (1)

it was like saying the wrong words a second time
in the room that was your bedroom also the one with the tv
where you ate with your mother
& up until a few months ago
the room with Sal smoking cigarettes after you got home from school
he said I'm leaving her
for good this time
which led to the rose petals & autumn
except nothing was pretty
& the red wasn't really red
just all over the bathroom
the heart so able to pump against gravity
defeated by razor thin lines
drawn deeply on her own skin like the veins of a leaf
happening three more times
until it was over

after her funeral
you went to live somewhere else
with people who were much older
but it didn't last more than a few weeks—
it was still fall
& the leaves were fluttering down
gathering under trees & in corners
sticking to wet pavement & floating in puddles

when Sal finally showed up
he hardly said a thing:
he looked bad
he smelled worse

something like a knife
was what was needed
particularly after he tried to kiss you on your mouth

EXODUS (2)

1.
she liked knives
especially after she had seen them laid out fancy
in a shop window—
metal
glinting in the sunlight
beating a two-count rhythm:
the small ebony blade she tried
at age eight
to steal—
silver filigree on
smooth ancient wood

walking straight through traffic
wicked & tall
loose on the night & the weeks
that barely unfolded into separate days
that knife's poor relation in her purse
earlier it had been strapped to her calf
its leather sheath tied under her soft black boots
but walking wouldn't do
for the strict unyielding
of knife
on skin

later he'll recognize this knife
not the way it'll be held

2.
she hasn't seen him in two weeks
yesterday at school Stevie told her where he said he'd be—
without Yvonne

alone on the subway platform
the wind through her coat
the rain
her feet numb & so cold

the doors on to the subway closing
open again
& slam shut
her arm / shoulder that time
caught
after the whistle
the impact harder than she would have thought
her body lurching heavily
indignant
sting of tears in her eyes

3.
something about the way she had stood an hour ago
made him stand in a similar fashion
except she had slid her weight on to her left foot
swung her hip round & poised

he had held his body still & leaned against the wall
laced his fingers through his hair
keeping his other hand wide open

she had bantered insults
laughed at him while he looked her over:
up & down
it was not the first time they had agreed on this take

now at her place
on the telephone
lying to Yvonne
his ante upped
her stockings & boots tossed into the air
as he watches
Yvonne or no Yvonne

4.
something of a false daybreak—
how birds chatter
alerted by the softening in the air
the smell & rustle of leaves as the wind pulls up
except it is too early
still many hours to come in the night
& the breeze is not what it seems—
a beginning
but from the middle of darkness
& this is always lost on the birds
who return to sleep
who decipher daybreak as a simple reaction
one song that summons light
as if a bird might conjure with its voice
misled by what it has seen every day—
light appearing
if not at this moment then in the next

5.
hitting the floor
in a heap
her shirt his leather belt
his jeans her panties peeled down & tangled
a hand on his chest feigning holding him back
their silhouette on the wall

he takes her hand & places it lower
she brings her hand back up towards his mouth

this is not my hair
these are not my fingernails
these earrings are too heavy for my ears
their sound out of sync
these lips hide under this flat mulberry colour
these thighs carry me into the next day unbidden
the spread between my legs
something you want
something I need back
from you
say the right words
about being here with me in my room
the second time this month
talk at me sweet
sugar my apple
teethe up on me
hold it
for me
nothing of Yvonne
whose name once aired
expands between the moaning sounds
rendering the air cold & flameless
begins a leaping waterfall in ice—
there are not enough words for the final rage:
I will not let you
betray me
the whole time thinking he wasn't wrong
to make his feelings clear
return the slap
again

then the knife came out—
lunging
she was angry boy
angry loud
what could he say to her now
as he slumps against the wall
already in shock
already nodding in agreement
her shrieks bringing someone else into the home
what has happened
not entirely clear
the knife's entry point clean
like flesh into flesh
pure
stainless
steel
time acute & no less fatal:

this
& this
now gone

EXODUS (3)

> *& the water that you take from the dry land is its blood*
> *walk across this land until you find water*
> *drink your fill & keep on walking*
> *come to me in celebration*
> *I am your God*

1.
this is what he has written on a paper he keeps in his suitcase
a suitcase abandoned to melt in the sun
now that he has scaled the wall to her building
gone through the two front doors
one always unlocked
the second kept open with a brick crumbling yellow dust
past the elevator sliding
& humming on command
reaching her 303 door with its eye & mouth
until there is only one other door
leading to air—
air that is dark
is grey
that on some days rides an aquamarine train
in total: five doors

the first time he was at her door he knelt down
put his lips against the metal
whispered a prayer
then knocked softly
but today is different
today is a desert that he has begun to walk across
released as if he were bringing the news of something lush & thriving

it is 8:15 eastern standard time
the weather reports no chance of rain

his fingers are curled behind his thumb & he is
hitting
hitting her door like a clock's second hand
pinned at one end
circling with the other—
all the numbers from 1 to 12 nudged gently

before dawn
he had taken his suitcase & delivered it to the sun—
his fingernails dirty
fingers hurting from tightly holding the handle
bent & swollen like earthworms adrift from land
he continues to knock
time marked in minute traces of blood—
the skin on his knuckles never so thin

2.
sometimes he does not sleep
sometimes he wants to sleep but has no place
lately he can not sleep

his head is clear though—
no more forgetting to board the bus
or once on the bus
forgetting to get off
so much time wasted
everyone knows the sand is hot in the desert
that you must find water

3.
on April 9th
1½ years ago
he asked her to meet him for coffee

84

I've seen you in church she said
you're about the same age as my first son maybe older
in fact he was five years older
eighteen years younger than she
together those years added up to his current age
a coincidence that he wrote on a napkin & put in his pocket
& later
after she had spelled out her name
had sat with him three Sundays straight aisle five
given him her phone number
he found a small red suitcase beside a cedar hedge
claimed it for his own
drawing a circle on an envelope lined with gold
he placed the three papers inside
snapped
everything into his suitcase

4.
peas & rice
peas & rice
peas & rice
please & rice
please the rice
a lapse at the dinner table
first last & only invite to taste her cooking
is there something wrong she had asked
& he told her I love you I love you
then dropped his face into his plate
came up blinking snowy rice
young Jeremy laughing
he said I love you
then reached for the peas & poured their honey into his mouth
warmth flooding over his lips licking

his shirt & peas on skin & Jeremy crying
he said I love you
& scooping up grapes
outstretched his hand
grapes cascading on to the table
spilling rolling violet
messengers he shouted with seed
she asked him to stop
what was wrong
was wrong what was he doing
she asked again & again
then she said: leave
which he did
pronto—
a definite lapse
week 18 of their courtship:
when the electricity wasn't aligned

5.
go to Montreal
go to Ste Anne de Beaupré
see the arm of the mother of Mary
on your knees
bear the cross
on your knees the stations of the cross

in Montreal
he delivered flyers
each one worth every penny
he returned:
cured

I am old enough to be your mother
join the young people's group
wash your clothes
call this number
get some help
come
we'll talk to Father Harrison
is what she said when he tried to apologize

6.
tried again to explain how the sun hurt his eyes
how hard it was to hold his head up
that he was hungry
that what he remembered when the noise
of mid-day
seared through his clothes
blistered his skin
hunted him down
past the solidness of a simple suitcase
was her smile

church she had thought
was no protection
so she asked him to stop sitting with her
stop speaking to her
stop thinking of her
stop

7.
it was October
the ground was too wet to sleep on
the benches too cold
trees almost bare

his clothes were not thick enough to keep him warm
not thick enough to stop the grinding sounds of the sun's movement
clawing at his skin
through the gaps in his coat

& he kept his distance
at church
on the street
behind her building
where once
a police officer kicked him twice maybe three times
he rode a bus to the east end
walked to a white & peeling warehouse
broken window hidden by tangled shrubs
lake in view
found 17 cardboard boxes
two slabs of insulation
eight wool blankets
enough mittens
socks
for one winter

followed by an early spring
a job cleaning
paying for a room
a prescription
oranges cereal
& he exercised
until July hit like a storm

out of that hollow clumsy silence
he returned
to love
the bible the same colour as his suitcase

8.
reading—
release after:
there is a drought
no water available to green up the lawns
perk up the flowers
swell the tomatoes

release after: there is a plague
to eat all the corn
eat all the wind
flatten the animals

release after: there are only stones falling from the clouds
stones breaking the branches
stone hurled against flesh
cutting
as he hides in the leaves of the night

after: now in place
he will never again acknowledge the sun
he will not let the light of the sun blind him anymore
he will not let it burn his shoulders
blacken his skin
deny the night—
it was always time to leave except
it can only happen once
today is that day
the sun behind him
the desert at his feet
the time: now

9.
he is at her door
carrying an earring
six pieces of silver cutlery
a cloth woven with gold thread embroidered in pearls
now that the wall is built
now that he understands the wall
why it had risen
watched from the bus as it ascended
blocking
her apartment
her window
only the flat roof in view
he knew there must not be a wall
that any wall can be scaled
this pink wall climbed easily five separate times this morning—
now at her door
without the papers
saying how her name must be spelled
how many years saying plus years plus the date
saying these seven numbers may be dialled but then minus age
uncarried to her

all in the suitcase
this suitcase held on to as if it were something of her
when only the space was her
that emptiness
that nothing
there must be nothing between him & her
she had said
absolutely nothing
zero

only the air
of two people
nothing between them but air
this suitcase found at dusk
the colour of dusk
all along a container for the thing he wanted most—
to be air
to be uncontained untrapped released into
beyond boundaries locks walls
circumventing words & meaning
only the breath that made the sound
so he offered the sun back its ruse:
gave back the shiny gold paper that held her name
gave back the fiery colour that held her numbers
gave back the vessel that hid cheated lied
surrounded the very air he needed
the trickster sun offered its own bag of tricks

this day was always his to be delivered into
this day his desert
his exodus

10.
& she opened her door
early enough in the morning not to think about who was knocking
& it did not matter too much that it was him
not too much
it had been such a long time since she had spoken with him
always leaving directly after church
not taking any time to look around
not wanting him to think there was something more
in what might be said
& except for the brightness of his eyes

everything was quiet
he smiled at her
& she asked him in
Jeremy at the table eating toast
toys lined up around his bowl
not remembering the man he had met a year ago
watching as his mother poured two cups of coffee

11.
the first thing he said was the bird must come with us
then he leapt from his chair spilling his coffee
& she knew this was a mistake
it was a mistake why hadn't she
& the bird was out
the cage on the floor
the bird high on the shelf
feathers fluttering & him cooing for the bird to come down
she took a deep breath & asked him something
so he'd have to
answer
maybe refocus
she could say—
come for a walk
let's get some
juice from the store

half listening he started emptying his jacket
saying this is what I have brought
this is what we will take
showing her the cloth the earring & the spoons forks & knives
then the bird took flight
startling him
made him reach his hand out to her
which she let go

just as fast
Jeremy now in the room & crying
for the bird
frantic
in its flight from light fixture to picture frame to table
for the sound of wings beating air
for the seeds now spilt the coffee & his mother's face
unfamiliar with fear
who in hearing her son
raised her voice
told the man he should leave right now
that it was wrong very wrong to come
which she hadn't meant to say
but did
& when he turned to look at her
she knew then what was going to happen
from her lips the smallest sound
time seeming to slow
she started towards the door
said to Jeremy
held one arm up to block the knife tried grabbing with the other
kept turning left to right to left
telling Jeremy to run
pushing Jeremy away
she knew she was shouting but her voice was far away
was she shouting?
she kicked him again
trying
trying to make him stop
she had the sleeve of his shirt but losing balance
fell
she hit her head
hard

93

& raising herself she felt her own smothering blood rush
& her head fell a second time
the wounds until then not too dangerous
not so numerous
but he didn't stop
couldn't
until the very air in the room was still
& the bird
huddled in the corner by the window
was tossed out on to the balcony to fly free
Jeremy silent
watching
it seemed to him
this man follow that bird into the sky
& not hearing anything
from anywhere
he lay down beside his mother
until there were many people hurrying around the room

12.
what happened what happened they kept saying
she in & out of consciousness
being reassured
mumbling her sons' names
over & over
sirens
faces
concern
it didn't take long for the ambulances to arrive
she & Jeremy taken together in the first one
bleeding & bleeding
haste not necessary for the other ambulance
a young man's fall
unbroken

94

13.
his locked suitcase
a lone figure at the edge of Lake Ontario
was found earlier
by young teenagers
who launched it out into the water
convinced it wouldn't sink

they followed its journey west
first on foot
then with their eyes
cheered by its buoyancy
watched as one bird alighted & rode the waves

they invented this bird
circling the sky always seeking a dry place

they imagined their bird spotting that small red island
then discovering:
a place without food
without water
slowly dampening
its sharp scowling cries heard by no one

lifting their arms up
they mimicked its plight
played at calling out
soaring & diving with enormous breadth

again & again their bird searched
this bird coming up empty
but coming through
green leafed clouds

green stones
breezes of thyme & wild blossom honey—

a tag of winged children
an island gloriously in view
each entrusted with the other
as the sun seemed to rise through the air